Notes on Disparity

Notes on Disparity

Alexandra Sashe

Shearsman Books

First published in the United Kingdom in 2025 by
Shearsman Books Ltd
PO Box 4239
Swindon
SN3 9FN

Shearsman Books Ltd Registered Office
30–31 St. James Place, Mangotsfield, Bristol BS16 9JB
(this address not for correspondence)

EU AUTHORISED REPRESENTATIVE:
Lightning Source France
1 Av. Johannes Gutenberg, 78310 Maurepas, France
Email: compliance@lightningsource.fr

www.shearsman.com

ISBN 978-1-84861-972-2

Contents

Introduction

These poems – which were put away in a drawer, one by one, as each of them came to life – are the most personal (and thus the most complex) of any I have written. I began working on them when I first came to Vienna, at the time when I was, properly speaking, discovering poetry, being so fortunate as to have entered right from the start that *purely poetic* dimension, where Art exists for itself, out of its own inner necessity, and is very exigent to those whom it introduces into its most secret premises. I had the privilege of being invisibly guided by one of truest hands in this field – that of Paul Celan.

The first piece of this collection – the poem *'Seuils'* (*thresholds* in French) came to me as an *opening*, as an answer to my literary quests, and – as a *door* into what would become my life and my poetry, quite different as it appears now from what I understood by life and by poetry at that time: for at that time I was still living in Paris, and was making attempts to write prose.

From then on, having definitively found my voice in poetry, I would come to Vienna once a year – to be there, to write that which wished to be written, to weave myself into its tissue, to let myself be changed by it – until, years later, unexpectedly, I moved to Austria altogether.

The leitmotiv of this first poem is that sudden encounter I made *in* and *with* the city of Vienna: *in,* in that I found there, as it were, distinct future traces of myself, manifesting their life through sensations, objects, visions and longings; *with,* in that the city imbued my soul with a feeling of *home,* previously unknown to me – in a place where I knew no one, where above all I did not seek to know anyone, and whose language I did not speak. And yet this was a place where I felt a vital need to remain, to belong to, to be part of – which would lead, in a span of just a few years, to my complete transformation.

The poem *'Seuils'*, as I was working on it, taught me to delve into the very matter (*materia; matière*) of Language, and *there* to look for and discern the hidden veins of poetics, and *there* to seek the vehicling force of poetry.

I felt that an unavoidable lot of an artist is an increasing if not mutism, then at least a certain aphetism and apocopism – for at some point, breath would be lacking, both through the excess of oxygen and through failing lungs.

(There exists a common misunderstanding that an artist works in order to express; or else, in order to transmit – a misunderstanding not unusual even among artists themselves. Yes, it must certainly be both – but only if an artist is not aware of doing either. The moment one tries to express or transmit something with purpose, and begins as it were to breathe consciously, one runs the risk of ceasing to be an artist – and the work, of being stillborn.)

And thus it was of necessity that the very first word of this poem, "*Lip-*" – which stands here for 'spoken', for 'speakable' – should be followed by the word '*-locked*'. This, however, I realised only much later, years after I had written this poem. The initial meaning of '*lip-locked*', the way it came to me as I was writing, had a more personal and a somewhat deeper sense – which I will come to in the Notes to this section. I mention this now only to give a small illustration of how little we are the authors of what we do, and how much we are taught and enlightened by what we seem to have ourselves created. And privileged we are, if we grasp, as early as in the very process of creation, even half of what lies in the depths, and then – continue humbly by ear, following that subtle yet clear sensation of what we *should* do, and obedient to that quiet voice that tells us what we *should not* do, i.e. *not* to shape it through our own, *already known* to us, ideas and thoughts.

Today, as I exit the field of poetry, distancing myself from what poetry has dictated to me, and drawing nearer towards What has been dictating to Poetry, this book needs to come to its completion. And so I settle now yet for a while in my present mutism (a happy crowning of what in my case seems to have been a poetic apocopism), not knowing whether I have ever transmitted or expressed anything – to think the first would have been rather a presumption; to have tried the second, a falsification.

All I can say is, looking at this book from a distance, it seems to me that it reflects what I could not possibly have intended to express – and least of all to transmit, I being scarcely conscious of it – the relationship an artist has with the creative force itself: how one lives by it, lives in it, and how at the same time *it* lives one, lives through one, lives one eventually into what one is meant to become, pointing *upwards* at its roots (for that is where all the roots are), its first source: Word, *Logos*.

The creative force has its own means in dealing with us – and only in rare cases it does it directly, as it was in the case of the Prophets. In our case, be it word or sound or paint, these are not the means in our hands, but rather we are the means of these means in the hands of our Creator. But it seems to me that poets, more than painters or composers, undergo the loving and violent impact of the creative force that pierces them through, transforming their being into its own material. For the Language is so intimately woven into our human fabric, that working on the Language cannot go without being worked upon by it in return. So that what one writes – and all the more, what a poet writes – is then hardly distinct from oneself.

But, with all the intimacy of this book, no reader could possibly feel transgressing my private territory. For, again, it is the Language that writes, and I am only its tool, a means of its expression. What it intends to transmit, through me, I will never know: the reader, remaining attentive to the layers of meaning which seem to unfold at almost every line, will certainly receive it. For there will be nothing "by chance", and no "bare coincidences", everything that the eye may bring to the surface, every association one may have and every connection one may spontaneously establish with oneself – all of this would be pertinent. The reason for it is simple – and this is true in regards to every artwork – in each particular case, we are confronted with out own personal poem or painting or piece of music, receiving what is meant to be conveyed to us personally.

*

The Notes at the end of the book should help – not so much in understanding what lies beneath *my* poem, but rather in offering more substance for (and a better access to) that *meta*poem which should unfold within the reader.

I am not keen on 'dissecting' works, if only because, as I have previously mentioned, we are not *quite* their authors. Nevertheless, in the Notes, I would like to make a few small 'incisions' – the way I have done here with the '*lip-locked*' – without altogether slicing into the matter, simply in order to establish the correct pace of reading, and to indicate the *width*, while the reader's own application and sharpness should help with the *depth*.

A.S.

We are in the very beginning, you see,
with a thousand things behind us and without act.

'Notes on the melody of things'
Rainer Maria Rilke

1.

Seuils

1.

Lip-locked,
place-ridden.

Happenstance casts
a cork anchor –
incision
into the closed parentheses

        (as chance may have it,
         may not,
         may leave it open –)

a painless surgery on the ever-
healing-over

eventlessness.
Counterfeit coins of days –
small change,
loose change:

alms to myself, begging
at the corners of long
afternoons.

Eye
caught up in reflections (mis)-
carries the *ever*
along the two-weeks' diameter,
sets in a circle of
monologues

a seal to one's lips'
partedness.

Full stop splits into colon:
casts the dice
to unlace the street lights,
to step in – barely leave
ruins,

(a shortcut of the
two weeks' radius).

Else,
to step out:
name – less,
initials, less –
a letter:

silhouette, mired
knee-deep in mirrors

                    (a static railway-ever-
                        go-round),

from here
into here in your side
vision
via the *Schwarzenberggasse.*

2.

Home relics
counterspell:

an essay proof-
read by a deaf hand,
sealed in, powdered with
dust.

At daybreak
waters lie seamless,
straitjacketed with eleven bridges.
One waits for winter,
face-prints on the pane.

Full stops crumble to marks of omission.

       (and the mist turns yesterday
       by osmosis. Yesterday hollow hours' holly minutes of
       Lent and Carnival, blood and roses).

Months siblings, hole-
bellied, – a
yellow light stutter at the crossing.
A monosyllabic stutter.
Place names,
lipped, silenced, are
locked away in the cupboards.
The stale yields no longer
to blade –

        crumbles
        to a forgetful sweep.

3.

Pivoted on desertion
the moons swing back – spill
over the cherry-striped coach.

Gypsies come,
predict your foresight,
carry away the moons –
leave behind
one
to play solitaire to
with your pack of *cartes blanches.*

Words-split, a greyhaired beetle,
is shaping
lips: open, closed, open
brackets.

      Awake, you see the railway slit
      your hemi-
      sphered vision.

2.

Aphetic

1.

*you*s thin out:

an open vowel
in common with the tree at the *Helmut* square,
                                                    autumnal.

elision from the acoustics
bound

for a yet deeper silence
in and behind the chestbones.

(home calls stutter
when what, when where…

: venation spells
an *O*-answer).

2.

…receding, it grows:
reinstates the magnetic power to the horizon –
a selfless green blotted out
by eye.

through the eyelashes
into the commonplace
winnow all
indestructible beings,
   their
            handcuffs and wings
are a sinkable surface :
unfastened they drown
and drown out
among the spells of the coffee grounds.

in the underhour, pillow
warm with your subconscious
estranged
into the static
game of shades.

at the *Helmut* square,
       beyond the season,
fog decomposes the souls free
from out the stone torsos.

upholstery lives by the dark
mother-relationship with hands and ashes,
healing each other away
from shapeless to sleepless
traces.

3.

All prayer
comes from and it goes towards
the in-front's vacancy.

All prayer.

3.

Homeostasis

1.

you's petiolated nearness

subsists on itself – till September,
the month's infinity sign
already wintry in the
                              deciduous memory.

the colour of a yet unknowable tweed
ages to light
towards the skin,
shades off the salt-
and-pepper, wood of violins, *you*'s ink,
its semi-colons.

                    an annual burial in the shallow
                    ever-weathering
                    soil.

                    (…other pledges and stone shoulders).

Atlas' fibre grafted upon
the warmth and the soleness
of sleeping body. (Unicorns are the guard cells of the
androgynous chambers) :

> a dreamt passage
> in and out
> the ultimate paramorphosis.

2.

distances accumulate
their unfamiliar,

entangle the threads of within and without,
figments of destinations
grow silent, yield
to their seasonal
autophagy of the obstacles.

rain's late envelopes
inscribed with pronouns
                          return birdwise
to sender:

                windowpane lives against and by
                its fidelity to
                the naked rain, chimes, cobbles.

        (at twilight condense other pledges and
        golden trefoil lockets).

clocks suspend their night communion
of breadful hands.

pendula's empty cradles
equate
the vicarious
blood and wine.

the chest of drawers contains the souls
who own their names, silver,
a measure of air, –
they are confessors of words damaged by water,
and sew upon
the rents in the ancestry.

     from the pages eyes
     carry away
     into the deep
     a little etheric treasure of madness.

     one learns from clothes
     to collect overnight
     non-violence, emptiness, folds.

3.

Dice at even
with fate,
untouched in the velour:

        the simple clauses of solehood
        make no use
        of the varied number
        of their omission points.   The smallest,
        the fullest stop, –
        thy single eye.

Conversion
on the instalment plan: a leap
at its codal *F major* syllable.

        Time is at hand and presses the grapes.

the written loosed from its meaning
goes back
on the spoken.

One may breathe. –
and wake up
freed of the speakable,
alone with one's voice
the colour of tweed.

the welcoming separating room
distills a 5 o'clock
from the figment of uni-
-verse,

inaugurates the seamline
for tearing apart.

One's self, bas-reliefed
among the renatal streets,
scoops its being by hours,
fills brimful
the quarter-centuries,

every morning performs
the descent
of the staircase,
conceives the dominical essence
of coffee, cello and piano.

(unicorns will come back
with the *Sonnenfels* lanterns and the trefoils,
gold and green,
of one's sole desire, –

inaugurate the scarline
of the will have been healed over).

Scarwards,
one walks into winter
behind the curtains of one's
emerald-green transparency.

The trees on the *Helmutplatz* justify
all withdrawals
regardless of depth.

4.

Apodosis

1.

A false-imposed arboreal lineage, –
an imposed sunshine,
                    names
interchangeable with pronouns:

        (the self-impregnating   self-sterilizing
        bondages).

a year-long view
over the gates of the garden.
impersonal tenderness of the branches:
                    an ivy principle of belonging, –
                    a homeopathic Garden.

        (So much for anything
        within the ever-
        -superimposed circles:
        encircling arms

                    again and again

                    falling short of
                    becoming vocal).

*you*s consummated
in breathless denials :
> the season of fruits and ripe
> idiomatic conclusions
> drawn towards
> the sole codal
> slender pirouette
> at the roads´ crossing.

Loose ends
caught up in the annual
rehearsal of open endings:
> a soft heartless fibre
> responsive as yet
> to a breath
> > to the scent of birth
> coming off from the dump foliage
> in each of the last but one recollections.

2.

birds' anonymous triangular bodies,
spindles, the white crows,
stretch out the yarn's
            empty stitches, –
            no appearance for no sake.

a bloodless
revolution of seasons.
home calls stutter : *"…so be …am here"*.
  The full-fledged phantoms, denizens of the Garden,
  ensemen its ever-
  -fallow soil.

            (cupped hands collecting
            the "*so*" the "*be*"
            in the conclusive abscission of letters).

3.

Wintry encounters:
may and cannot.

(a false-imposed lineage, ever-barren,
of the incestuous cardboard characters).

Oracle's hands,
sieves of the time particles,
                again and again –
                and ever –

                                scoop and
                                pass empty

                through all
                space.

5.

Homecoming

1.

subsists in the peripheral eyesight :
a naked branch is forgiveness.   *Helmutplatz* recollects
its winter. A silence-bearing season.

>   its bread,
>   a sweet-astringent kernel, is
>   bearer of April.

The home is one, and the hearth is spared
the non-inflammable ink and paper,
ersatz ashes and harmless
mist in lungs.

So remains
the *you*s disavowal, –
homonyms
under the layers
   of the frozen unechoing pavement.

>   A cornerstone waits for the eyes, outspoken, –
>   for the sake of the sole
>   consonant.

A less-than-one, a narrow doorway
to the inhabited
rooms of the timeless. Mirror, Clotho's face,
weaves its own measure-made
anthropomorphic eternity.
                    (Parquette's tactile sense,
                    a prefiguration of weightless steps).

2.

frost
auscultates the souls
without transgression:
walls' interiority keeps at home

        the souls' linens and faces,
        the linens' and faces' pledges.

porch is threshold,
unfolded margin. –
In the month of Mount Tabor
the salt of the winter rain
bears the name
of the river Tabor.

3.

      One snowflake departs southwards.

The chimes of the northern belfry
release its anastatic doves,
the patron saints of the thaw.

Age, exempt from the ways of the eyes, –
its surface
retains no fingerprints.
                 Age,
a virgin with her ever-lit
oil lamp.

The church steeple –
the first who grows older

         (its bird-pad and fog-pad
         tucked under, –

         its language
         mutilated forgotten).

4.

city
a mount summit.
the true hands contain a harbour
of their being beyond age.
Maundy morning tastes of honey and dead
sounds.   The true hands are partition
and are
the cleansed leper's hands.

6.

Interlude

1.

a windless *Helmutplatz*
testifies
towards the eternal
      the meta-arboreal,

           our self-accomplished silence
           pregnant with our
           single self.

the garment of our testimony
 is broken in
and makes us to measure:

           our hands pass
           the ordeal by ice.

         a respite hour of the sunlight
         heals away the *yous'* anaesthesia,
         the wound-field of their thesaurus
         narrows, closes and skins
                    over.

(The wood of the floor recognizes
  the weightless steps
  of one's adoption.)

2.

the rain overcoat and snow overcoat
grow their snowgreen and raingreen
                                    leaves
and reasons for being.

          in our wardrobe
          they sleep and meet
          their unshared purposes.

                    (leaves and clothes,
                    a common degree
                    above the naked:

                    one grows, –
and grows into shedding
clothes)

          A retrospect ear distils the pronouns
          into alliteration:
                         our pavement, laid
                         with the estranged camouflage,
                         is swept

breath by breath,
dawn by dawn.

(the unleavened silence of our rooms
is, with closed eyes,
our guardian).

3.

(It is March that sows and harvests
im Amberg.
And the wings of my strength offer a feather,
a tear, a fresco heaven
         for the feast of the metanoesis).

Home deducts revelations
from the clocks' and the coffee beans'
inter-reliance.
                              Snow melts
                                        and lends
                         the windowpane
                         its fingers.

4.

A pedestrian month
of April and mercy.

the city lives back, away from its youthhood,
the boulevard circle
bestows its leafage
                    upon the naked
                    espoused confidence.

A limpid unseen unspeakable
path
fire-trodden, paved
with relics.

            At home one sleeps and kneels
            at the strait gates
                        wide open.

7.

Heimat

1.

Land-locked
tongues step-mothers
ridden with chestnut leaves,
with planes and ashes.

a table surface
focal plexus
of eyes and branches,

         Helmutplatz.

Enclaves of daylight, archipelagos, –
one's re-entries
at soleness island:

A city flays
and the city skins over
with her motherly step-adoption.

      (Conditional tense, an orphan from birth,
        lives by himself
        on bitter herbs

an orphan from birth with burnt hands,
soothes his burns
with bitter herbs).

(Subjunctive vision,
a figure at twilight,
close-open-closes
its white overcoat
of self-exegesis, self-pardon and
                              self-disappearance).

2.

La rue Madame, ruins' radius,
alive with echoes, with soul's shuttle,
with one centripetal vector,
with window envelopes, –
    with awaiting in retrospect.

  A long light,
  pages explained by its length,
  collected by handfuls:
  a brewage of coffee and clocks,
  of disburdened pain, of seasons'
  invisible
  escarpment.

3.

Days bells
inaugurate
the daily fulfilment of time,

its units
fast among
prayers and vigils,
immolated and safe
                    and lit
by our common sun.

With our being we profess
the corn of wheat
            and a lineal future. –

(Ahead of its coming,
  we ask and wait
  for the single word).

4.

Blessed with the thirst
and the kingdom
of April and acquiescence

we enter its breath,
resurrected
       henceforth
transparent to our touch.

It breathes us in –
       and we know its name,
       we drink from its tear

   and are permeated

        with its

      healing transparency.

Notes to the text

1. *Seuils*

As I have mentioned in the Introduction, the word '*Lip*' initially stood for the spoken, the speakable. While the expression '*lip-locked*' only echoes 'land-locked', the word *'place'* affirms it (and the final poem, *Heimat*, finally confirms this association, for it starts indeed with "*Land-locked…*").

And so, being lip-locked in a manner of a land, alone with no access to water, surrounded by other languages / lands / (…), one soon comes to feels *place*-ridden – with that vibrant and unresponsive inner space, on the one hand; and on the other hand, with those vast language- / land- / human-spaces, which have no reference to one's own: spaces where an encounter is but a *cork anchor*, which doesn't ground but remains instead on the surface, even though, true, it is life-saving…

"*Lip-locked*" and "*-ridden*", while conveying a state of muteness, will perhaps give it a nuance of suffocation, of being overcharged: with Language as a reining power; with languages as an overpowering and unremitting experience; and finally – with lands as a frame for both.

"*silhouette, mired / knee-deep in mirrors…*"

I worked on this poem on my first two successive stays in Vienna, mostly in the *Café Schwarzenberg*, whose great, tall windows give on to a busy square continuously crossed by tram-lines and pedestrians; inside, the walls are covered with mirrors. This created an effect of permanent intersections of inside and outside, of reversed movement and multiplying dimensions – which in its turn created a sensation of a certain environmental, and almost existential, tautology.

This also explains the last verses of the first and third parts of the poem.

"Home relics / counterspell"
– the second part of the poem was written in Paris, upon my return. The word *'home'* thus translates not that mysterious feeling I mentioned in the Introduction, but bears its literal, somewhat down-to-earth, meaning: with the word *counterspell* testifying to it – for (without my running the risk of dissecting, as it lies on the surface) the double meaning of the word *'spell'* cannot slip past one's eye.

2. Aphetic

This chapter was written during my third stay in Vienna.

The word *'aphesis'* means *elision*, the loss of the initial unstressed vowel of a word. Here it alludes, by extension, to one's impaired capacity of naming; the elision is that of the initial capital letter with which a name starts, thus reducing a personal name to a generic one. But more specifically, aphesis is the loss of a *vowel*: I shall speak of it more at length in the Notes to the chapter *Homecoming*.

Here, the Language – as a vehicle for one's thinking, a ground of one's perception and understanding – comes into better focus. The opening line, *"yous thin out"* sets the theme which will be developed in the following chapters: the inherent distance between human beings, a *pronominal* mode of their relationship (*yous*, having a multiple usage and losing their uniqueness, individuality, eventually come to imply their replaceability)…

(The line serving for an epigraph to this book, is taken from 'Notes on the melody of things' by Rilke. There he speaks of it much better than I).

The last verse of the first part, without disclosing the very personal intimate *reference,* should at least succeed in conveying the *sensation*: the voices from home, confused, anxious, calling back – produce in one's soul, dwelling in its inner aphesis, only *"an O-answer".* 'O', apart from being a letter of the alphabet (for me also, the initial of a name of a person), has a visual '0' [zero] reading to it, as well an audio *'No'* [a-no-answer] sounding.

Helmutplatz, which will reappear later, here and in some of my other poems, was at that time in the centre of my intimate relationship with the city.

"fog decomposes the souls free / from out the stone torsos."
– Atlases, the mythological characters that hold the skies upon their shoulders, are often used as architectural embellishment. They are a remarkable feature of Vienna: often lifelike, with their personal physiognomic identity, they seem to live a life of their own.

"the in-front's vacancy"
– should be understood, of course, not as the addressee, but as a condition for a prayer: solitude, isolation, reclusion; alone with oneself, in one's *lonesomeness,* one encounters one's *oneness,* that *inner solitude* where a wordless prayer is born: born not as an act, an instance, but as a form of being, and finally as a state. And so, this external solitude as its first condition, the *'in-front vacancy',* remains its most natural element: prayer needs it and cherishes it, and, in so far as it *'goes towards it',* it prays, as it were, for itself, in order to be.

For some time, at a later stage, I thought of substituting *'beyond'* for *'towards'* – and indeed so should it be, at a later stage: born from this solitude, it must be that prayer overcomes it, and lives *beyond* it.

3. Homoeostasis

This chapter was written during my fourth and last of my yearly visits to Vienna, when I was still unaware that I would leave the city without leaving it, and return to Paris without ever returning – and that in less than a year I would move to Austria on a permanent basis.

Homoeostasis is perhaps the most melancholic and elliptic piece. This *current of inner time* where images, sensations and revelations come together in an ebb-and-tide motion, should be distinguished from what is commonly called 'a stream of consciousness'. Rather, it is a passive, contemplative introspection. In the time of working on this poem I lived closely among those images and sensations who came to visit me and of whom I was by no means the origin. This contemplative dialogue felt much like glimpses into *the memory of the future*. And indeed, now looking back, I see that many of them turned out to be prophetic.

The botanical theme, having already appeared in the previous chapter, here weaves into the theme of language: Language as being inseparable from its source, the Word – the Word that names, that creates; the botanical theme as that of growth, of renewal – of a rebirth as a promise of a final, lineal, eternal continuity.

The opening line, *'you's petiolated nearness'*, takes up the thread of the previous chapter: the *pronominal* mode of human relationship, that subsists as it is, unless a superior, divine force interferes, restoring one's unique *I* accomplished in the unique *you*.

'month's eternity sign…':
August is the 8th month of the year, the digit 8 (oriented horizontally) becomes the sign of infinity

'guard cells' – (*bot.*) cells that surround the airway pores of the plants, "guarding" their capacity to breathe.

'paramorphosis'
– following the pattern of the word 'metamorphosis' *(Greek)*, where *meta-* means *change* and *morphe* means *form*. Here the prefix *para- (Greek)*, (i.e. *going beyond*), helps to construct a word to mean *going beyond form, leaving behind the notion of form.*

'autophagy'
– *(Greek)* in anatomy, the capacity of cells to devour other cells, those which are dysfunctional, ill or unnecessary.

'thy single eye'
– cf. Mt. 6:22

'unicorns (…) sole desire'
– an allusion to a series of medieval tapestries 'The Lady and the Unicorn' (Paris, Musée de Cluny), each piece representing one of the senses – vision, hearing, etc. – except the last tapestry, which bears a title *'À mon seul désir'* ('*To my only desire*').

4. Apodosis

This chapter was written the same year as the previous one, upon my return to Paris. Feeling myself more and more estranged from this city, which I nevertheless loved, it seemed to me that Paris, for its part, was more and more "estranging me" from itself: I was walking away and it did nothing to hold me back. This tearing apart was both its own pain and its own anaesthesia.

Apodosis
– *(Greek)* in the Eastern Orthodox liturgy, the last day of an Afterfeast.

"Oracle's hands"
– alludes to the eponymous poem, from my collection *Antibodies*.

5. Homecoming

This chapter belongs to the first year of my life in Austria, the year that saw the beginning of my spiritual conversion. Indeed, the name Österreich [Austria], in the way I spontaneously translated it in my mind, would offer me the path and show me the destination: *Oster Reich*, the Realm of Easter, as distinct from the "Eastern Realm" of Österreich.

The word "April" should be read in this context.

"for the sake of the sole consonant"
– I use the word *'consonant'*, here and elsewhere, with a double meaning: first, as a designation of what my ear perceives of *consent*; the second signification goes back to texts of the Patristic era – *consonant* symbolizing the voice of reason, in its opposition to *vowel* as a voice of the spirit. Also, here, a few lines above, in *"so remains / the yous' disavowal"*, the word *'disavowal'* would echo a *'vowel'*, thus linking both meanings. It is to this latter meaning that the word *'outspoken'* (as an image of an open vowel) wants to point.

Clotho
– in Greek mythology, one of the three sisters, Fates, who were in charge of human destiny and life: the first span the thread of life; the second measured it; and the third cut it off, whereby the life was ended. Clotho was the youngest, the first of the sisters: she is usually portrayed with very long hair, which she is weaving. The image that is the vehicle for my thought here comes from a sculpture of Clotho by Camille Claudel, which I saw in Paris in Musée Rodin: a very old naked woman,

completely bald.

Auscultation
– a medical examination, carried out by listening to the sounds within the body, as e.g. a doctor would listen to the noises in one's chest and thereby make diagnosis of the lungs.

"In the month of Mount Tabor"
– Mount Tabor, besides its proper biblical meaning (the Mountain of Transfiguration), alludes to a place in Vienna – the *Taborstrasse* – where I lived at the time of working on this piece and where most significant *transformations* took place.

"anastatic doves, / the patron saints of the thaw"
– *ana-statis (Greek)* would mean revival, rebirth, re-being.

"a virgin with her ever-lit / oil lamp"
– see the parable of ten virgins (cf. Mt. 25:1-13)

6. interlude

"our hands pass / the ordeal by ice"
– In the Middle Ages there existed a practice of ordeal by fire, a trial that sought to establish or disprove the innocence of a person accused of a crime. The accused had to hold a red-hot iron rod or a piece of burning wood, etc., and – in case of their innocence – it was supposed that the accused would remain unscathed.

In my poems, *ice* usually has only one meaning: coldness, indifference.

"It is March that sows and harvests / im Amberg."
This entire verse, even though referring to something very personal, is however not hermetic. March being the month

where the feast of Annunciation is celebrated, the '*wings*' are those of the Archangel Gabriel.

metanoesis
– the term *metanoia (Greek)* literally meaning a change of one's mind, of one's way of thinking and being. In the New Testament it is commonly translated as *conversion*.

"at the strait gates / wide open"
– cf. Mt. 7:14

7. Heimat

Heimat
– in German this word means '*home*', but implies something deeper, more fundamental than what is commonly meant by the English word *home*.

"with chestnut leaves, / with planes and ashes"
– chestnut trees came to symbolise Paris for me; plane trees both Paris and Vienna, although curiously more Vienna than Paris; and finally, ash trees – only and intimately, Vienna.

Of course, the word "ash" reads clearly in its double sense, where this second meaning in turn also has its ramification: *ashes*, being what is left after burning (here, the leaving and burning of bridges), and also, as an old symbol of penitence: penitence that opens into liberation (just like the winter solstice, being the darkest day of the year, indicates the beginning of an increase in light, so that Ash Wednesday, marking the beginning of Lent, means the beginning of spring, of life's renewal, of one's re-birth).

In many places, and in its prosody above all, this poem sends the reader back to the first piece *"Seuils"*. Though this book should not be thought of as a *circular* literary work.

"the corn of wheat"
– cf. Jn.12:24

www.ingramcontent.com/pod-product-compliance
Lightning Source LLC
Chambersburg PA
CBHW050023090426
42734CB00021B/3388